FREIGHT TRAINS

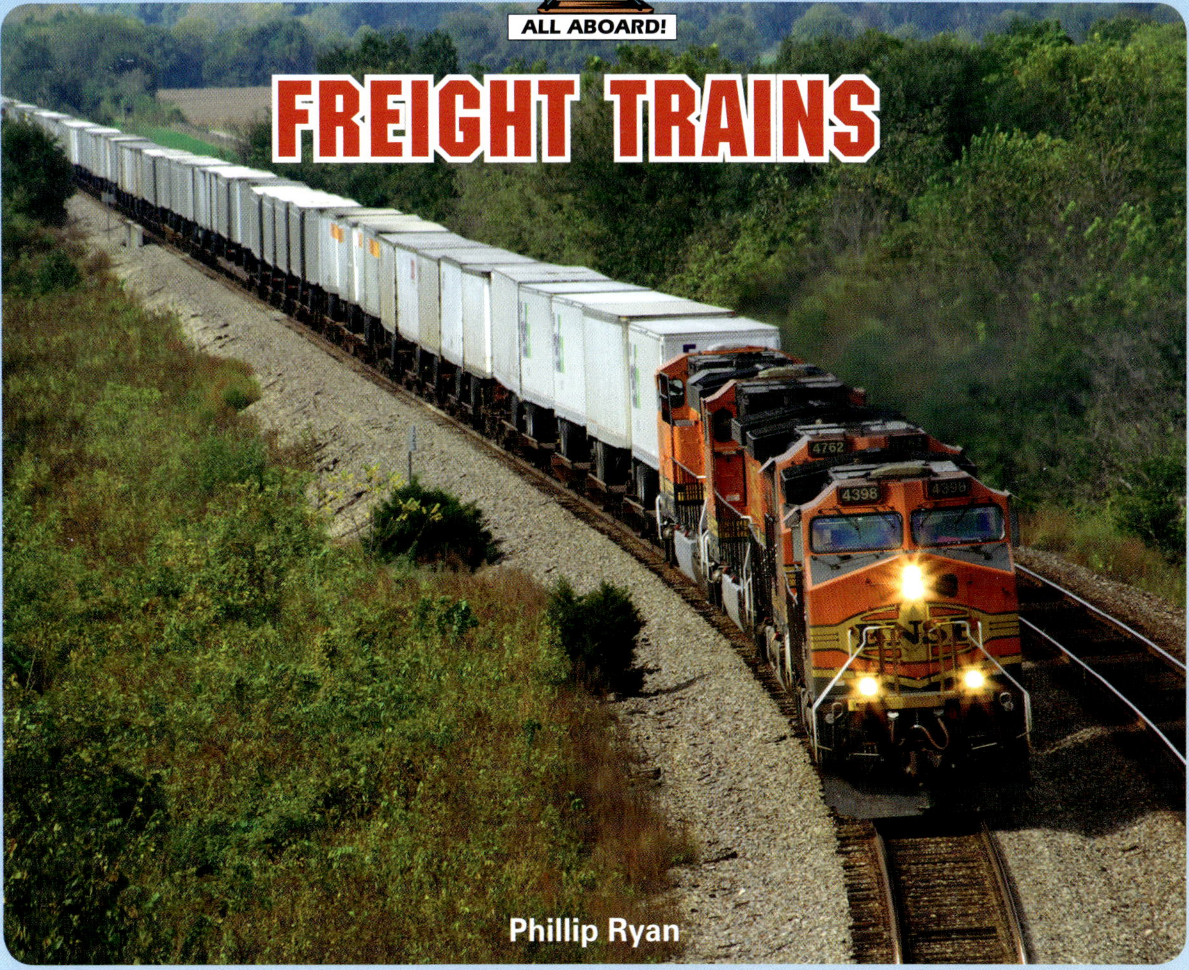

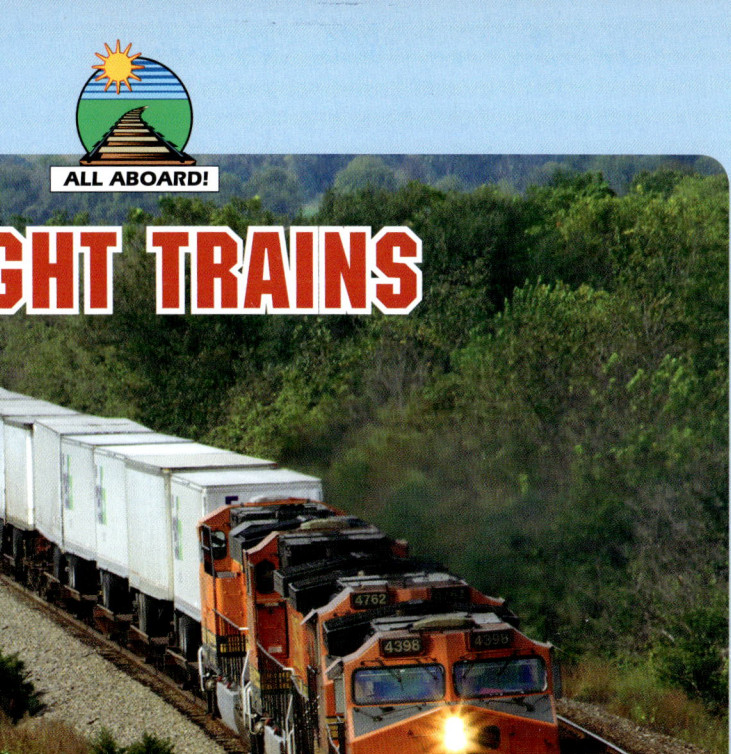

Phillip Ryan

PowerKiDS press
New York

Published in 2011 by The Rosen Publishing Group, Inc.
29 East 21st Street, New York, NY 10010

Copyright © 2011 by The Rosen Publishing Group, Inc.

All rights reserved. No part of this book may be reproduced in any form without permission in writing from the publisher, except by a reviewer.

First Edition

Editor: Joanne Randolph
Book Design: Ashley Burrell
Photo Researcher: Jessica Gerweck

Photo Credits: Cover, pp. 5–15, 18–19 Shutterstock.com; p. 17–18 © www.iStockphoto.com/Eddy Lund; p. 21 © www.iStockphoto.com/Vincent Bernard; p. 22–23 © www.iStockphoto.com/Imre Cikajlo.

Library of Congress Cataloging-in-Publication Data

Ryan, Phillip.
　Freight trains / Phillip Ryan.
　　p. cm. — (All aboard!)
　Includes index.
　ISBN 978-1-4488-0635-5 (library binding) — ISBN 978-1-4488-1211-0 (pbk.) — ISBN 978-1-4488-1212-7 (6-pack)
　1. Railroads—Juvenile literature. 2. Freight cars—Juvenile literature. I. Title.
TF148.R936 2010
385'.24—dc22

2009048610

Manufactured in the United States of America

CPSIA Compliance Information: Batch #WS10PK: For Further Information contact Rosen Publishing, New York, New York at 1-800-237-9932

CONTENTS

All About Freight Trains 4
Parts of a Freight Train 8
Freight Trains Everywhere 18
Busy Freight Trains 22
Words to Know 24
Index 24
Web Sites 24

Here comes a **freight** train rolling down the track.

Freight trains have a job to do. This one carries **coal**.

6

The load a train carries is called freight. This train carries goods inside big boxes.

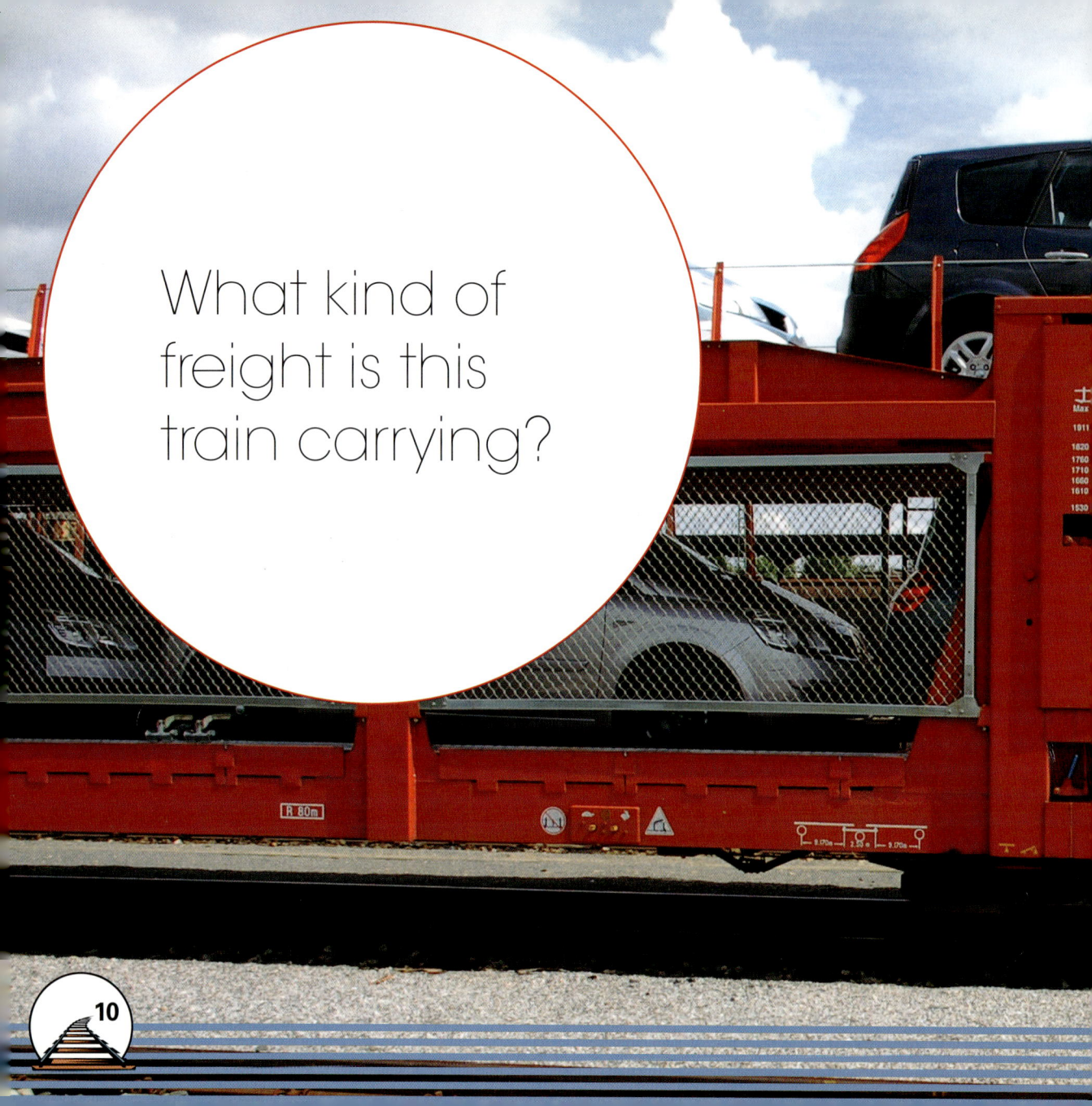

What kind of freight is this train carrying?

Freight trains roll down the tracks on **wheels**.

Freight trains are made up of many parts. These parts are called cars.

The first car on a freight train is called the **engine**. The engine pulls the load.

Freight trains carry loads in many places. This one rolls out of the hills.

This freight train is pulling its load across a bridge.

No matter what they carry or where they are, freight trains are always busy!

22

WORDS TO KNOW

coal

 engine

freight

 wheels

INDEX

C
car(s), 14, 16

F
freight, 8, 10

T
track(s), 4, 12

W
wheels, 12

WEB SITES

Due to the changing nature of Internet links, PowerKids Press has developed an online list of Web sites related to the subject of this book. This site is updated regularly. Please use this link to access the list:
www.powerkidslinks.com/allabrd/ft/